green

green

marilyn bowering

TORONTO

Exile Editions

2007

OVER 30 YEARS OF PUBLISHING

Library and Archives Canada Cataloguing in Publication

Bowering, Marilyn, 1949-

Green / Marilyn Bowering.

Poems.

ISBN 978-1-55096-094-5

I. Title.

PS8553.O9G74 2007   C811'.54   C2007-901445-3

The cover drawing *Rose* by PK Page is reproduced by permission of the artist.

The author thanks the Canada Council for its financial assistance during the writing of some of these poems.

Design and Composition by Homunculus ReproSet
Typeset in Cochin, Bembo and Mariposa at the Moons of Jupiter Studios
Author photograph by Michael Elcock
Printed in Canada by Gauvin Imprimerie

The publisher would like to acknowledge the financial assistance of
the Canada Council for the Arts and the Ontario Arts Council.

 Conseil des Arts **Canada Council**
du Canada   for the Arts

ONTARIO ARTS COUNCIL
CONSEIL DES ARTS DE L'ONTARIO

First published in Canada in 2007 by Exile Editions Ltd.
144483 Southgate Road 14
General Delivery
Holstein, Ontario, N0G 2A0
info@exileeditions.com
www.ExileEditions.com

Canadian Sales & Distribution:
McArthur & Company
c/o Harper Collins
1995 Markham Road
Toronto, ON M1B 5M8
toll free: 1 800 387 0117

U.S. Sales & Distribution:
Independent Publishers Group
814 North Franklin Street
Chicago, IL 60610
www.ipgbook.com
toll free: 1 800 888 4741

for PK

for M and X

Green oh how I love you green.
Green wind, green boughs.
Ship on the sea.
Horse on the mountain.

LORCA

CONTENTS

green

tell me

near

metaphysics

stopping by

coats

green

Once I knew a cave—
you and I have spoken of it—

you arrived there
out of the dark,

you carried a charred stick.

My bare feet slipped
on wet stone,

my eyes met the gloss
of your eyes—

what other world could there be?

We held hands
like lost children—

though we were not lost,
we had found the cave

where we might make anything

and wait for the light
of another time.

What marvels of sound,
of water,

of the brisk stirred air
of bat flight:

my breath was your breath
my dreams were yours,

even when the great jaws
of the rising sun

devoured the dawn
of our beginning.

When I used to dream,
there was a house:

it didn't belong to me,
but all night I stood
in its wind and rain
like a window

against which
a bat trembled,

and I sang
to the house
that belonged to someone else:

I was not ruled,
unless it was by sadness
that I would not see you again

with the wind writing words
on yellow paper
as I approached a wall.

Who *are*
these pilgrims,
wet-booted,
hair streaming,

hands on their throats
—Aii!—like a cry
about to born

in battle?

A dream would know
the geography.

Now there is peace
of the kind that longing brings:

sleeplessness,
long halts

as I stand on the driveway
broom in hand, not sweeping.

I listen to the trees:

what do they say
but *green green?*

At last I understand Lorca!
Verde que te quiero verde.

And remember his life in cities
and the cafés
and with his friends hidden
by night;

but most of all
it's the sweetness of Granada I recall,
even the terrible barranco at Viznar,
full of sedge grasses,

a blue hyacinth its only flower,
where exhausted murderers tried
to eradicate poetry:

Ay amor
Que se fue y no vino!...
Ay amor
Que se fue por el aire!

Why think of such sadness?

It flourishes in the bodies
of those we love;
it also needs joy.

Only the dim light of stars,
and the faint black of trees,

and the stirring hangers
in the closet,

and the ghosts that cross
in slippers —

some bright
as polished spurs —

defend the room
that is ours.

The rattle at the door,
the scrape of a chair,

the tongue as it searches
the mouth —

all these are a prayer,

or like the wind
as it writes letters in air —

everything unsaid
but sent —

like yesterday's travel,
or the patterned footsteps of mice,

like nothing on earth
but a bright meadow.

Give me your cup
so I may break it,

give me your hand
so when it leaves mine,

I'll know its loss.

All of it: knife and fork,
garden spade, clean sheets
on the line —

let them fall.

There is a place —
I do believe it —

where I'm at rest:

I come with nothing,
leave with nothing.

Let me go —
like this teaspoon of sugar
as you stir it,

or like the ashes of the dead
strewn over azaleas
and at the foot of totems —

so that I can be present
in fragments: or like a poem

where there is stillness
in the containment of a word.

I could start drinking again
just to know an empty bottle;

I could return
to certain doorways, the sound
of a bell that tolled,

the movement of slaves, room to room;

I could go out into rain
and undress
and feel nothing but needles of cold,

and lie down under a plastic coat
in a strand of trees
just back of the road,

and listen through a chorus of coughing breath
for word of you.

The night hums
along its yellow line,

its survey tape of the mind —

(some always know
how to find this path).

I could wait like a simulacrum,
like a clothes-peg doll,

I could unfold letters
for mention
of a name,

and swim at night
in a ghost lake,
my legs green with weed;

and the dead hands
that touch there —

I've never told
of their reach,

the twist of knowledge
like a screw of sugar,

far inside
where I can't remember.

I could take a candle,
if one should appear,
and make it last

just to see your eyes,
just to see your eyes,

and the stars are our knives,
and the bitter cold of the night,
and the strangeness of your getting up,

your clothing like the rags of an army
your hands untying my bones
so I cannot follow

shivering my way
through keys:

and I'm undone
when it should be better than this —

not this dark landscape
not the architecture of fate —

but a kiss to take us out
of this terrible land.

Remove this dress
and beneath that

the underdress,
and beneath it

whatever you find —
I don't need it.

Then the skin,
layer by layer,

all bands of muscle,
and tissue — whatever it contains —

lay it aside —
I need no protection:

and if you find
a heart,

don't be gentle
cast it ahead

to see what follows,
if anything lives

that is my concern.

When I used to wake,
I'd fall from a dream:

the bed caught me,
its lathes and softness

made me turn to you,
your skin my skin.

Then, there were the stars,
their sharp 3:00 a.m. voices,

the specific tremor
from each constellation

as the bed slowly swung
on its planet platform.

When I used to wake,

I didn't know that I peered
through an envelope of breath

at the window,
the black spear-points of trees;

that the stars
sparked inside me because I breathed;

that my waking was their waking,
their fall, mine,

although I heard the splash,
on the other side.

I open the zipper
of the body,

fill your lungs
with the sound

of rain,

separate planks
of bone,

spread flakes and shards on tarpaulin,
snap them into bags

and freeze them.

I sample
the DNA of lost pages,

build a model,

circulate your picture
in the private black hole

of data,

track the green
of grass frozen in permafrost,

dissect your last meal,
am familiar with anthropod and icthus,

the astreus and estrus of shed
vertebrae —

everything I do belongs
to the ages.

I know your handprint
and footprint, the lick of your tongue

on salt; I know the fur that adheres
to tendon, I know you in part,

and by nature,

my hands are full
of your desiccation.

I send an arrow across the gulf—
that's history;

archaeology is a glimpse of you
through blinding snow.

I undress
or don skins,
build a shrine
of human bones,

and still all I have
is a museum.

How to bring you alive
and keep you in my arms,
bring my heart peace?

Let time answer the question.

If I have a home,
it is far away:

I'm about to set out.
The compass says 'up' —

but who can trust
base magnetism!

My poems are my suitcase —
none of value, none
that need to be declared:

who will stop me,
only a woman,
with this luggage?

I want nothing held back
especially the truth·
of your absence.

I *could* imagine an intersect,
an apex of an angle —
that's about it —

some star, all fire:

let's waste no more time —
if you're coming, come.

tell me

What!
Writing about the dead, again, Marilyn?
Put on your shoes, reach the meadow.

The dead are here too? What?
Don't you know where you are?

Can you name what you see
without falling snow,

or the washed dish of sun,

or the worn table-top of rock,
or the songs wrung from air

and set to billow their colours
in the wind? Yes colours: those birds

that flutter through the laundry.

What? You're no washerwoman?
Not so! Don't you scrub clean,

don't you begin again, and again,
like a star or a field mouse?

That grain, carried from the wheat-field,
how do you think it began?

Somebody walking, their hands free.

Tell me about memory: is it a problem
of translation?

Is it a footstep,
or the striking hand of a voice

through your faithlessness?

If you know the name of a flower,
then you must describe its colour,

number the petals, explain the basal leaves
and the stony soil, the sun-baked mountain slope,

the difficulty of the climb to reach it,
your companions,

the loss of a stone on the way,
the curve of river in the scraped plain,

that stone, again, still falling towards it...

What! You recall no trees,
no cloud like a hammer

descending on this steep of mountain?
Aren't you afraid of the smash?

Did you feel no blow?

How about the passing of strangers,
the shuddering of your blood?

Your unfittedness

is a scandal: why don't you scream —
and above all, what are you doing here?

How dare you assess this flower
without love? Too much?

Makes you weep? Then don't begin,

put down that notebook,
close your eyes,

but don't think I'll let you rest
until you say my name.

Canyon

I can walk the canyon trail,
listen to the squawk of branches

high enough on their stalks
I might think they bend

for me, but their talk is of sky,

or if not, the missing birds: damn
missing birds: what else is there to do

on a bright spring day, the air pinked
with snow? There has to be

something to look forward to. I can
sniff the dung of plants,

the path deep over roots, fir needles, stuff
happening a million times,

that is, everything's layered: the river

like a slice of green melon
between the still-frame motion

of stone: what happened here? A push
from below, a first second

and third thought about what the earth is made for;

an ordinary tumble from the edge—

like my heart tumbles
when I'm not looking. Oh my—

it's the way I forget
the night, how it wraps this up—

a little walk like an animal,
blood thumping because

it must.

Night talk

Like the caravans of traders,
everything is happy to begin:

even the sheets and pillows
are gathering points of movement.

That man crouching beside the river,
is dreaming of carriages, of the woods

at night, the whisper of leaves falling
to cushion his way.

He hears the glass hoof beats of horses,
the thin pines trembling

at the carriages' passing.

How often I've been there with him
in the dimness, talking

while he takes off his clothes
and enters the water.

Talk to me, talk to me.
until it is summer

and our cries reach
the riverbank

and everyone else who is waiting.

You are not compelled by the dead
although the dead move room by room

rearranging the flowers, turning down
the gas, opening the windows.

They want what is best for their unfurnished
lives, for their small flames of love.

You may complete their stories,
but they are not your stories.

See here! You're a child in a schoolroom
watching horses in a field. Pay attention.

The horses *are* more lovely,
than anything. Where will they take you?

Do you ask the question,
or do you just go?

Life seems colourless in comparison
to imaginings of immortality —

those hand-coloured pages, colour-washed
gold and silver letters.

Delicate tendril and leaf create the illusion
of a world inhabited by spirit

though Nature has no form
but the wind slipping between the slats

of closed blinds.

Still, no part of me won't see the sun rise
or question the window. What's kept out,

what in?

It's as if a room is a woodcut,
and upon its walls turn

the pages of a multiple view,
and the unconscious resonates.

When I brush my hair,
the mirror holds two bodies.

It's a complex magnetic field
and the texture of flesh

overlies the symbolic.
(That mirror — a parfait!)

Freud says the primordial experience of living
is close to a haunting.

(A kind of underground palace
accompanies language in dreams,

and the greatest achievement is the resurrection
of the dead speech of symbols.)

This isn't rational; what room is when you think
it's peopled by the unseen?

Like the night tremble of a hand
through my hair, it's nothing to do with me,

but fulfils an irreducible need of the human soul
to become part of a pantheon — that is,

like a school of fish, beautiful and violent,
that controls the life of individual fish.

Little within this world is known to my reason.

But I have to ask: how can a symbolical rose do
what the rose itself cannot —

decide to be beautiful?

Perhaps it does not depend on the medium,
but is an expression to be construed as evidence of design? —

like a hand is a design, or a blinding reflection
is a reference to light.

Like the destruction of selfhood enables
a real self to come into being. Yes?

When unconscious halves meet
there's a collision of awakening

that might be a conversation with paradise.

(If I'm to be honest, it's too revolutionary
for my processes of thought.)

But everything that lives is holy —
isn't that the intuition? — seen or unseen? —

like the walking shadows of lion and lamb,
the blowing petals of rose and sunflower;

like the tatter of wind through a closed window,
as it becomes the emergent contours of a body.

near

What shall I do with my love of poetry?
Shall I give it to you, who will think it a stone,
keep it in your pocket to test your fingers?

The moon is round, like a lover's nipples —
and see how the stone leaves your hand
to pierce the pure air?

What shall I do with my love of poetry if you
tear it into words, as if bread for birds
whose clapping bills seize on disappointment?

My love of poetry is the dark room of my childhood.
Its passing cars light up the windows
and freeze my eyes open as an entire wood
turns its pages across the ceiling.

What shall I do with my love of poetry?
My love of poetry takes to the road —
it has dangerous eyes,
its roe breasts are the twins of desire:

do not stop for it: it will ignite your longing
and despair —

and why not: when it has me by the throat,
and its free hand roams my pockets for stones
and it stands at the window
looking in, greedy for entrance.

What remains of the wood?
Ash.
What remains of the river?
Stone.
What remains of the night?
Dark.

Oh gateway—who is at the entrance?
Oh gateway—who holds the door?

The night is a black bird
on the rooftop,
a button in its beak,
under a clear sky.

For the rooftop
there is no gate,

for the river
there is no depth,

for the star
there is no darkness.

I crouch over this paper,
the wind flames it in my hand,
its ink is a black wave
that sands a shore.

How you lie, hand and foot
bound with a thread.
before the tide.

How long will you wait
to untie your hands
and read?

I dreamed a room,
I dreamed it was a beginning,
I dreamed I awoke
and saw the prison,

its oceans and skies,
the dome of enclosure.

Am I a stone that I do not feel?
Am I winter that my medium is ice?
Can I endure like a forest?

I am this moment only, a breath, your words,
the time when
anything can happen.

Let me turn the key in the lock
but first let me feel it in my hand.

When I remember to look at them,
the oak leaves are the tiny palms
of imaginary beings: those that I hold in my arms,
whose olive-grey heads lie against my breast.

When I remember they are there,
I am careful how I speak:
nothing loud or hurtful,
bird song, maybe, the evening plaint of song sparrows
and the gentle questions of warblers.

When I remember to forget
my heart's leaden fist, its thump
against the door,
an emblem—well, a key!—appears—
if I could only remember to take hold,
allow its work.

You who I hold in my arms,
who I sometimes remember,
forgetting that I have made you up
from the air of my longing:
I know how you love me,
the way we have nested like this
in the fire-swept cracks of mountains:

how well I know your footfall
burned into the earth.

If I could remember
a world that brushes my hands as I walk,
my lips when I consider water,
and become salamander, adapt,

I could learn to love this fire
the sound of its syllables in the words you'd say
if you were near,
when you are near,
now.

The night's cup over a bowl of prairie grass—

take away the yellow
and the night blackens

like a river in a valley,

like a feather seen through a window
that goes click against the light.

The horizon spits lightning,
an owl slams into wind—

but in a boy's room
it is morning, and I've just begun

my search.

Take away the city in which the boy lives,
the blue duvet under which he sleeps,

his mother going out the door.

Take away me just waking up in the Franciscan friary
with this dream awash in my breast

as the horizon readies a break
into the clay of a hot prairie day.

In the boy's bedroom, I'm still opening a drawer.
If I recall what I find,

I'll know why I go to the window,
look out and discover the bird on the rooftop—

its iridescent blue wings,
black breast,

the red sewing of its beak.
Did I mention the cage?

Who knew
what the boy kept hidden?

Take away coyotes that yip the thread
of dawn, the bell that wrenches the brothers

to prayer.
Did I say wrench?

The poem says, notice the bird's imprisonment,
and the boy's name *Francis*...

The chapel is empty,
wind walks its walkways.

(Brother Michael, his bones like scars
beneath his brown clothes,

his back like a curved tempered beak,
slips into the chair beside me.)

Dreams are dreams, the poem decides to remind me,
and they speak to you sideways —

Brother Michael, I say in my heart,
do you know the bird too?

*Now I know what I took from the drawer,
what shall I do with the key?*

Advice for the twenty-first century

When I'm alone, and I remember to ask
at twelve midnight, and at the stroke of 3:00 a.m.,

I'm at some threshold
with a million others,

and the summer fires in the forest
are only light, not pain,

and the world is a murmur of electricity
through the silence.

The house is two countries, only one underfoot;
and the documents and photographs on the table

spring to life, full of hope,
and my longing becomes happiness.

How precious the sweetness of empty night,
and at the same time, the dust quivers

and I want to wash my hands again and again in clean water
and think only of those peacefully sleeping.

(I hear you shout: the weather is all green!
We're discussing meaning and I can't sleep.)

So many wounded: every morning the count
is a white pistol shot through my dreams.

Get up, tell about the wreckage —
tell whoever will listen

about all those drunk on technology —

although even they can't muzzle the bees
or the trees and streams or gravity,

or climb through the smallest black hole —

and we all want honey and clear skies,
and we're going to cry out

when we're loved.

I will never reach the sea
ahead of the arrival of waves:

it can't be done

even by drones searching out targets
with their red mosquito bites of infrared:

don't let them silence our pillow talk.
It's better when I don't think.

How hard everyone tries not to think.
Don't try so hard, walk upright

like a human being:

don't trample the gardens
with hooves you don't have.

You were sleeping as the dead sleep
in the hilltop grasses, yellow with sun.

Rain and wind and all that passes
had passed: you were quiet as clouds,

your heart riven with seed,
your flesh an eruption of flowers.

When I considered you, it was as
the unremarkable days I pass

without you: all that was deep
in me had shut: think of the earth

over time, its embedded pre-history
turned to stone; and think of the seas

disappeared from continents; and a door
in a story that can never be found.

In this tale, I stand at the door:
I hear your cries, and my answering shout of delight —

and the knife of it becomes my spindle again,
and I have to live.

metaphysics

Metaphysics I

I phoned the hospital to find You:
You weren't there.

I said, I'll call the Others.
They said: there is no other but Me.

I went away — really away —
not just the usual

thoughtful shopping

(what else is there to do with the painful,
and metaphysical?):

You feel like Time,
not like love's sweetness:

that's why I'm lost — I count by You,
rising and setting,

I talk about You
in the cafés, as if I had a life

with

my hands, Your mouth
your hands My mouth.

Metaphysics II

If you say *prick* people have certain thoughts,
language folk, your dearest friends, all strangers —

the kind you depend on

to get things right. They know the fucking names
of everything, even if they fucking don't.

So, at night, when I lie down, there's this pricking —
I'm wired end to end — a flock of migrating birds

has found a short-cut — me — to the other birds;
or maybe I'm empty space, a rare non-habitant,

the world's easement? Hello, hello — do I know
any of you?

There are: whistles, whispers, puffs,
breath, held breath, full-length freight trains:

and you wonder why I don't sleep?
Am I worried, grief-ridden, lost, found,

drugged, not-drugged? God damn it, no!
Just a corridor, somebody's home for a moment,

conducting thousands. Not that I mind,
since I can't stop looking

for you.

Metaphysics III

Time is a black shoulder bag
that carries a heavy stone.

Consider it an ally, listen:

a dog is in prison;
it knows nothing

of the night, but the night
knows it.

The dog is your restlessness
opening and closing windows.

Don't pretend
it isn't you. Your dog can't disguise

your predations,
your howls,

your thumbprints
tracking through waste-ground.

The night (on the other hand) is the owl's
swoop. Sleepless one—

leave your handbag on the shore
for the dog,

pass into the ecstasy of deep water
and drown.

Metaphysics IV

My heart is a river.

Outside its bending walls —

the theatre of traffic,
the broad division of roads.

My heart wears a green dress,

it wears the night
as its footprints.

How wide the shoreline
where we swim

heart to heart.
on the way

to the originating sea.

Metaphysics V

When I think about the grey space I've found
like a tunnel inside a worm,

its silvery sides glistening,
and the absence there of the vivid world —

its tree growth or babies
like sun apples or the jewelled skin

of a frog or the tiny snapping sticks
of the forest under the feet of the predator,

and the scrape of sand along skin
when I'm caught and pushed

in the Pacific — and I also recall

your mouth and its desperate speech
your loss and loss and loss, then

a word does form and it's oh and
its signal of blue is like

a port — perhaps Le Havre —
which I love for its light-bracketed

river, the sense of flow the inevitability
of tide,

the absence of *no* when I observe from the deck
a ship's arrival and departure — oh — in this

grey physical space where I keep
the accompaniment of heart and its memory

and I'm turned towards birth —

I imagine it could be (that) you'll be there when I emerge;
and if in the silver and grey of the worm-sides,

the unexpected interior camera-
oscura view of new space, if *there*

why not *here* in the frost-cracked winter,
the shattered mirror of my life?

Metaphysics VI

I could say I understand *the dark, like a fine web of silk,*
but this lie would stop me greeting the surprise

of my departure from the woods of dream
in a season when snow covers the earth's curves,

and the waterfowl paddle forth, paddle forth
shadowed by wings

amazed at such temerity.

Your eyes are a break in the dark;
you come from the frozen reaches;

you're a ghostly web
crawling over me,

my lost passport.

I roll out from under you again,
yes again!

Metaphysics VII

Despite our accounts of reality,
there is love,
just as there is

music without sound,
music of the imagination.

But who set the innocent on board that death ship?
Quien sabe?

Undo your nighttime tangling,
unwind the stars:

now you know how to play, can you listen?

stopping by

1.

If you could stop a train
you could be happy for a moment.
But don't ever count on happiness —
it's unfaithful — in fact,
it's unnatural!

Like that train under the sun
chewing the grass — how natural is that?
You see, it thinks it's spring (warm earth etc.) —
but it's a stranger from mountainous places
you can't even guess at.

Let's be calm about it:
it's a feeling I have when
I've thought and walked:
when I die, the day I lie down,
it will be with the poetry of night
layering the grass, swamping the lamplit windows

and beginning to come alive again,
like a stopped train
lifting its head
to contemplate a miracle.

2.

Hello, you wearer of sunglasses:
hello you bearer of swords:

you're not the wind,
you're not even a column of ants;
you're heavy and peripheral but

many times, it's my fault
and other things — those memories,
those lapses and soul failings —
they take many forms,

perhaps

you're not as overt as the wind,
the wind that never stops blowing,
still
I forget what I had to forget
to become you.

3.

Ants again, and birds —
those feathers, those braided leggings!
I dance the *lambada*, but only
in my dreams where
no one looks at me.

Mostly I'm reserved and won't dance
at all,

but I remember Mother Nature —
Mother Nature in all her naturalness —
what love she had to embrace me!

Pass on birds, pass on ants, bye bye.
Bye bye. Bye bye:

I'll always remember you.

4.

Who thinks to mine fossils in a wood?
Don't you know about hope? Can't you sniff it
in trees that have vaulted into tiny clefts
of soil? And some of you arrive in four-wheel drives
and ATVs with rugs and thermoses and lawn chairs—

and somebody has to carry out the trash—on his back!—
to the dump.

When will metaphysicians help with that work, I ask you!
It's an esoteric question, don't dismiss it.

I wouldn't need to remark on these things
if you'd help me out. Ouch, everything hurts:

especially my eyes, near evening,
when the world is roaring pointlessly.

5.

And then there are poets who draw,
and writers who sing backwards,
and carpenters who nail legs to the tops
of tables:
it's so sad to smell flowers
in a world constructed of walls.
I can't tear down anything: it's all nailed
shut! The earth is a case of art gone mad:
too much variety, and everything the same.

Just think about it, just think and breathe
as if you were a flower or a horse;
do you understand me?
(Nobody understands me.)
This conundrum
creates a divide.

How delicious you are! Living earth,
you levitate throughout the solar system
and you're happy to do so.
No wind rocks you to sleep.
You are just, without shadow or cloud.

6.

I'm late. In *ad hominum* reference,
crickets cross the threshold;
I've left the door open just for them.
Sometimes ladybugs make nests
in the window corners.
I'm looking for
a softening of operations, that's all.
I dress up, I attend the opera:
I know how to pass muster;
I own many things.

But I've forgotten too much,
even my suffering.
Everything is as important as everything else:
the crickets, the ladybugs, the young singers
immured (in walls), long go, so that someone
(I've forgotten who) would be recalled.
Imagine such small imaginings — as specific as flowers
or rags. My soul repeats and repeats, like a Mynah.

God help me to bury my ego in flowers,
or in the two rivers that run near my house.
In winter they swell and cannot be crossed;
in summer they're useless,
I'm preoccupied, clearly.

Some good-looking man, full of potential,
walks by — Love — is it a crime?

7.

What wouldn't I give for a life in the woods!
Wait a minute, I live in the woods—that is,
the forest leans against my windows,
birds approach the barrettes in my hair.
The woman who cleans the house is pale,
she holds the ladder steady
while I climb to the top and swish a wet sponge
across the glass—*swish*—no more evidence of
in and out: I've eliminated here and there.

My hair straggles over my neck: my car
needs washing: no horses range my backyard
and yet—I still think I'm going somewhere,
even though I shout the fundamental:
what am I supposed to do?
Well, what? Say thank you?

What I wouldn't give for a life in the woods
(I still say),
deeply hidden from myself.

8.

I'm following a period of instruction
even though I'm remembering the butterflies
on the grid road in Saskatchewan: how was it then?
Sunshine, a weight on my shoulders,
red butterflies in *touch and go* on the gravel—
How is it now? My heart is numb:
no perfume or flowers or butterflies.
How can this be? Every flower needs to bloom.

Like a great blotch of fog—that's me
under the table: I refuse to come out.
Seems a bad way to continue: I'll be late
for my life. Calm down: you'll appear and
disappear. You're like a swimmer in a lake,
surfacing for air, or diving deep.

Those instructions? To drink water,
think of flowers, wash the scent of myself
out of my body.

9.

Write this down: I'm standing at your shoulder.
I've taken off my clothes.
I want this to be natural: put away your
camcorder.
Before I feel you sizzling in me,
I have to know your absence. Its presence
by absence, if you know what I mean.
This isn't metaphysical: it's as real as the shoes
beside the chair, and the Mynah bird in the room
shouting, Mynd your Manners!
I'm naked: I'm full of ideas: I'm about to swim
out the window, graze in the grass
and sky,
move contrary to Nature: I don't know
what to do
with this passage of my soul through the night.

You weren't listening when I said
I won't go this way alone.

10.

I've had any number of cars,
some of them friends: but my best friends
are the dogs who never forget me.
Everyone else — pffft! — out of sight etc.
I'm out of my mind with forgetfulness,
that's the truth: only the dogs with good noses
can find me.

11.

Thank god I'm not perfect: how could I stand myself?
My faults give me work: people in general like
to consider my errors. The world is gracious:
Make a mess of things? That's okay, so does everyone else.
Have a good laugh; one day you'll discover your imagination
has taken you for a long cold walk.

Wait a minute! I remember how it started!
I wanted to live in the woods, and by steep-walled-gorge
look where I've ended up! My family — mostly dead —
my lovers — what can I say? — my children —
permanently absent. Ah, all those sentiments —
sometimes I feel
my hands touch a thread.

12.

Let me listen for you, a moment:
I am afraid of nothing but drowning.
I always let you have the lamp.
It's been three nights since I've slept.

So, what's up? I'm to what? Remember
you're there?

I want to get drunk, eat myself into stiffness,
refuse to sleep for a month. Who cares if I'm a bad example?
I've done this before when nothing stops the hurt.

But listen, even so, my heart lies down for you,
it suggests a time and place. What do you have to say?
Where can we meet?

13.

Stopping by woods and hills.

14.

Like a too large borrowed suit,
once again I demonstrate my unfittedness:
what's underneath? Scrawny bones,
dumb posture. Actually, I'm happy
to be born, but it's time to get out.
Ad nauseum or *ad-vent.*

If they say I don't know how to live,
just examine my leavings: empty bottles,
and suits, coats, bird cages: to live is to
think about the mysticism of cars —

what do I like? Top down whizzing through
the green forest, rain slicing like wood grain,
the air sawn by skull, cartilage, cheekbones,
hands clenched to the leather-jacketed
wheel —

What a ride! My body's a mess,
I've missed everyone I've loved,
nonetheless, their love piles up
in me
like a car wreck: I'm a one-woman
demolition, not at the end of the road,
though I can see the last couple
of turns,
and
overhead, switching through branches —
crows, ravens, eagles, tiny humming birds
and the Mynah cawing hello and murmuring
nothing sweet...

my nostrils stinging with dust,
foot to the floor as if I
must take off —

but, still,
I'd rather be here, on the backroads,
summiting slash and deer-stitched paths,
then just looking back with heartache.

coats

1.

I open the closet door,
and my mother's cloak
falls into my arms —

as if it were herself
emerging from the dark corners
of the unseen and unworn.

She thought life would dress her
in brilliance. She cried out —
How lucky to be alive!

A swing of black cape
with red-silk lining...

I take the cloak and spread it over my lap,
spy the ragged stitches
where she tried — late, late — to mend,

and thread red silk through a needle's eye,
my head bent to the work,
to join with her intent.

2.

This morning I watch a deer,
heavy muscled, black-tailed,
confront our cat who raises
a tentative paw, sits back on her haunches.

The deer resumes
nibbling green tips —

the cat springs.

(Who's more surprised? —
the cat when the deer leaps off to the woods,

or the dog, crouched further back,
who finds it now safe to bark?)

What coat should I wear
for an epiphany about assumptions?

Perhaps the long black tailored one,
with a button-in lining?

But it's for winter,
when the view is demented with rain,

the bushes stripped, the grass pale
and mouldering, for when drizzle stipples the glass

and I quaver, hands in pockets, in this coat
which is the best I can do to look civilized

at funerals.

My mother said it was a beautiful coat.
So be it — beauty then:

it's a must for when the balance of large and small,
habit and thought is trimmed. I need practice, that's all,

in remembering.

3.

Is it too soon to talk about
the community of coats?

Where do they come from?
Whom do they seek?

They line up,
winter and spring;

they're how I tell time...

the yellow trench,
the Salvation Army Harris tweed worn while pregnant;
the parka from Corniche in Edinburgh
(my favourite)...

They come out at night, imprinted with scent.
They touch hem and cuffs, babble in tongues:

made separate, seasonal,
long to be

One.

4.

Coats fly out of the closet—
Gogol's overcoat, Jacob's dream-coat—

and I see that I haven't considered metaphysics—
where do coats (imaginative or real) go?

I examine forensic evidence:
strands of hair on a collar,
chocolate in pockets,

stains in the lining where lovers
have lain in the snow...

Coats escape, find new identities at the
Sally Ann,

end up as rags, or thrown out
in that final move to the condo, return to dust,

dust of our dust, a lost earring
caught on the thread of a hem.

These coats—messages to the world that say,
Take me as I am.

5.

Let's say that life's journey is not round,
as we've been told,

but point to point—like that doeskin jacket
on a hanger and its broad (apparently) shoulders.

It's been worn

by a woman (me) who has, shall we say,
her own angles,

and there are slopes and curves,
puffed pockets. Never mind:

the idea is that squares interlock—
like the tangle of hangers in this

clogged cupboard, only better:
begin at Alpheratz, say, travel to Scheat,
Markab, to Algenib, and home.

From the Great Square,
jump to Andromeda,

go to and fro on bisected angles,
the radii, to Mirach, Almach,
to M32, and then,
to escape geometry,

once and for all, leap to a spiral...

like, in a way, I change my mind,
take out the old ski jacket now, because

poof—it's the wrong season for deerskin.
There was a reason for beginning

and it was
the deer's skull in the bonfire
in the backyard,

and that once, after the tenants left,
I found a deer, stretched out, dead
under the porch —

a last resort, or maybe the nearest thing
to a cave in arboreal forest —

and my ten-year-old and I dragged it
to the wood where now also lie

beloved Raphael and Bluebell —
and if I have my way, I will too

when I let go of all these coats
—let fly —

and be at home in green earth
or up there, in the ancient mines
of the sky,

for what's above is as below.

Once, we too were force
and formless:

this coat is a shape that fits
what it finds in nature:

square, circle, the single dot
of the hunter's bullet.

Hold — while I say a prayer
for the deaths that have brought me
comfort.

6.

The closet swells. The bees that have been skating
the hallway window die. Are some killed

by sun? Too much of anything
causes pain. I see the dark bodies of coats

as I go in and out, each one calling:
Me, take me! like querulous children.

You could starve in there, grow lean
and threadbare. Enough. I keep what I want—

many coats—

like a people who tell their stories in knots,
or the self-effacing, confident only in that

they *inhabit.* I name the contents,
clean up afterwards the easy way,

sweep clear the windowsill of bees,
shut the door.

7.

Chagall liked coats: wide sleeved,
with flying tails — and those top hats!

(The top shelf's overrun with bonnets — but I won't start.)

My mother's navy wool overcoat knows
the art: of course it could soar over rooftops,
naturally flight's an aspect —

— all those theatrical
swatches of paint and fabric —
poor Chagall. He lifted off,
felt faint. Left for Paris.

Her beige trench coat's a classic,
sighs on its hanger — *When
will it rain?* The coat's too big,
who did she think she was? A giant?

I find a list in the pocket:
her life's in her *hand*,
each stroke of the pen

a hieroglyph of time, place —
flight!

8.

I've been thinking about that dream coat of Joseph's,
and about Chagall, and mothers:
of the origins of the wish
for splendour;

and means of travel,
like the flying carpet,

that allow the world to unfold
like a white handkerchief;

for rivers and streams and foothills,
for the mountains and waterfalls,
for deserts and tents of
refreshment

to appear,
for the city of Mecca
to be found beyond a hill,

for Jerusalem the golden
and Byzantium, as well,

for the man and woman and child
who will enfold you

to be kept in secret,
in a handkerchief,
in a pocket of a coat

that you acquire at a thrift store
or from someone you love,
or that belongs to the secret world
of someone you love,

for the coats in the closet
to be signals of far-off lands;
wool and silk and polyester,
leather and cotton — just think

of the places and people and all the human
involvement: like that old Harris tweed —
so old it *was* made on Harris —
the women who waulked the cloth for it
singing:

This is not cloth for priest or cleric,
But it is cloth for my own little Donald of love,
For my companion beloved, for John of joy,
And for Muriel of loveliest hue.

9.

It's summertime:
not a coat in sight.

Even at night
there's no need:

the river glistens
under blue light.

Travellers take pictures;
dancers sweat,

their skins like
ripe persimmon,

their breathing —
sweet mulberry.

I move through the world
on a whim — heat-soaked, slow,

the house far away and locked.
There'll come a time, no doubt,

to open the door, call out,
Anyone home?

The planet Mars slips
near: red and gold,

burning its hot eye
into the dry hillsides.

I flinch,
not from cold,

but the thought that all this
like a pale veil,
or snow,
or a fine coat,
will thin.

10.

Seven coats like seven winds:
who cares? But the closet
won't be contained.
As if I'd climbed that hill
always visible
and seen, far below — Mecca —

and was caught in a whirlwind
that brought me my father's puffy jacket.
I know it by the short arms, his jaunty
grin as we snapped it closed around him,
all his women, and he as king —

these things stick, some would say
an aura clings, but it's more the story
of the body and mind, adhering in the fit.

Oh wind of sorrow, I've hardly touched
my mother's coats and jackets, plumbed the pockets,
watched her walk away in low heels and slacks,

climb the hill, with me, as she would —
that wind turns me again and again —

must be a reason —
I hunch in Michael's leather,
push aside the pristine golfing jacket
am shaken by his scent —

love's a wind of the senses, even here, on a bleak hill
in an alien land, with strangers who take my arms,
as if to lead on...

This wind brings tears,
a classic case of the desert and its need —
seeds germinate and bloom in seconds —
a glory of colour —
I'm the odd one out in this chain of gardeners,

but I can thirst for ecstasy; like a whoosh
of this warm air it lifts me high, so high no people
remain, and the hills are the curves of a beloved body,

and we're in bed, making love,
a fleece on top for warmth.

Seven winds, and more coats than I can number
with these blurred eyes (my father's grey raincoat,
and look — Maya's wet suit!)

...and all the coats of my ancestors,
all the care that weighs me,
all that tags space with our names,
each hair,
(DNA)

Whoosh!

Coda

Good morning fellow travellers!
It's a beautiful fall morning, this morning;

it's a beautiful morning everywhere
trees grow, leaves colour the wind,

the animals of the forest forage —
the Word says they shall not be disappointed

for God visits the thankful — and the animals shoulder
their burden of riches and go forth.

It is a beautiful fall morning,
the atmosphere is singing.

The air of the wood is vivid
with bird song:

life's work continues —
a making according to form,

square, level, honest,
of good material, and sound.

Good morning fellow travellers!
You shall not be disappointed!

Your burden of love or sadness,

is a leaf on a wind
that scours the desert tracks:

seeds are blown clear across
unnavigable oceans and begin.

I have news! People rise up with wings
as angels. There is reunion!

As I, even I, stand before you
finished,
and draw into myself
the woods,
the singing.

Notes and Acknowledgements

The Lorca epigraph is from a translation by Will Kirkland in *Federico Garcia Lorca, Collected Poems*, edited by Christopher Maurer, Farrar Straus Giroux, NY 1991.

green:
When I used to dream was published in *Quills Magazine*, Vol. I, No. 3
When I used to wake was published in *The Malahat Review*, Fall 2005, No. 148
Some of the poems in *green* have been published in art post-card form by Pooka Press
Remove this dress and *I open the zipper* were published in *Event*, Vol. 35, No. 2

tell me:
What, Tell me about memory, Canyon and *You are not compelled by the dead* can be found in the *Banff Centre Anthology* published by littlefishcartpress.

near:
What remains of the wood was published in *Event*, Vol. 35, No. 2
Advice for the twenty-first century is, in part, an homage to Lorca

metaphysics:
Metaphysics II was published in *The New Quarterly*, Issue No. 102

stopping by:
The entire poem was published in *Exile The Literary Quarterly*, Vol. 30, No. 1

coats:
Coats was published in *Exile The Literary Quarterly*, Vol. 28, No. 2
The song in *Coats #8* is from *Carmina Gadelica*, Alexander Carmichael Vol. 1 pg 307

Dedications

Canyon is for Don MacKay

The night's cup is for Nicole Brossard

You were sleeping as the dead sleep is for Phil Hall

Good morning fellow travellers is a collaboration with, and in memory of, Herbert Bowering

From the point of view of the rose is for PK Page

Appendix

From the point of view of the rose,
the bird on its way to its nest
is of no consequence.

The bee, on the other hand,
draws the geometry of sweetness
flower to flower:

distances sway
according to the wind
of an intricate innate ballet:

Only the bird perceives the rose totally.

Put science aside: or bring it close, as if the microscope
and spectrum telescope were the fine hairs
of the bee's belly, its organs of dalliance —

here's the romance of attraction, the plus and minus
of eye contact, the medium of brain

like some primordial soup: creation's about to start
and I'm here, keening,

As not everyone who reads a leaf knows its meaning.

Upturned cup, leaves incised on a hip,
is as good as any means to assess
this attempt to scry the rose,

its scent at one with fingertip:

and look — I'm ready at once — without a shove! —
to dive into the heart: you're my oxygen
it's as deep down here as heaven above,

O you who from the book of reason would see the signs of love.

Books! I meant to reference botanical text,
the knife of dissection,

to lead you by degrees
to tear the rose as I instruct:

but — attention deficit be damned — the essay's lurched
out of my hands:
all I can think,

my senses assailed by love,
is how scant the hours, how profound the dove.

*(I fear that you cannot fathom this subtlety
by research.)*

* *From the Point of view of the rose*: the four italicized lines are
by Hafiz.

info@exileeditions.com   www.ExileEditions.com